Little Business Books

Teamwork

Written by **Ruth Percival**

Illustrated by **Dean Gray**

W

FRANKLIN WATTS

LONDON • SYDNEY

First published in Great Britain in 2024
by Hodder & Stoughton

Copyright © Hodder & Stoughton Limited, 2024

Credits
Series Editor: Amy Pimperton
Series Designer: Peter Scoulding
Consultant: Philippa Anderson
Philippa Anderson has a business degree and is a writer
and communications consultant who advises multinationals.
She authors and contributes to business books.

HB ISBN: 978 1 4451 8571 2
PB ISBN: 978 1 4451 8572 9

Printed in Dubai

Franklin Watts
An imprint of
Hachette Children's Group
Part of Hodder & Stoughton
Carmelite House
50 Victoria Embankment
London EC4Y 0DZ

An Hachette UK Company

www.hachette.co.uk
www.hachettechildrens.co.uk

Contents

What is teamwork?

Teamwork means working together.

You need others to play games, such as hide-and-seek. A choir sounds great when they sing together. A football team works together to score goals and win a match.

Good teamwork needs skills, such as listening to others and doing things in a fair way.

Why does teamwork matter?

In business, teamwork is very important. It might mean trusting others to do a good job or solving a problem together.

For you, teamwork might be working as a class on a big project or being part of a sports team.

What will our animal friends find out about teamwork in business and about themselves?

Be a good leader

Things are about to go wrong at Monkey Adventures!

Team B sent a customer, Leon Lion, the wrong way around the zip wire course. Leon Lion and Kiki Koala are about to crash! Their team leader, Milly Monkey, stays calm.

Everybody, stop!

Milly Monkey helps her teams to work together to fix the problem.

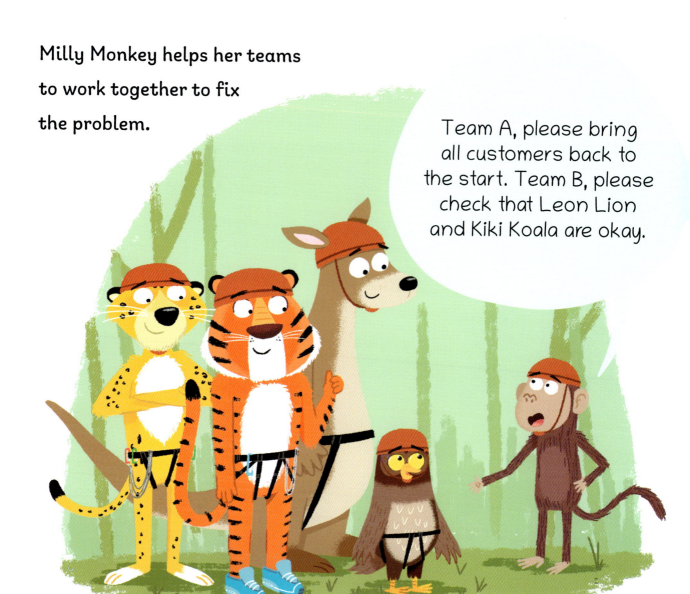

Team A, please bring all customers back to the start. Team B, please check that Leon Lion and Kiki Koala are okay.

A good team leader stays calm when things go wrong.

Feel motivated

Today, Pip Penguin's team is not working hard.

They don't feel motivated to find new customers.

But Pip has a way to encourage them ...

If you find ten new customers today, you can leave work early!

Peggy Polar Bear and Peter Panda spring into action!

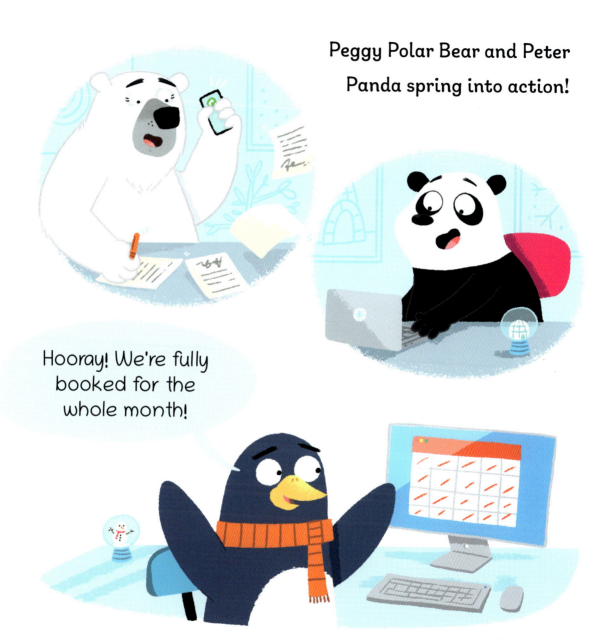

Hooray! We're fully booked for the whole month!

Motivation can make a team work harder.

Ask for help

Enzo Elephant is very busy. Owning a toy shop means he has to do EVERYTHING by himself ... or does it?

Enzo Elephant asks
Wei Wolf to help.

As well as serving customers, can you open and close the shop every day, too?

Wei is happy to have more responsibility.

Enzo is glad he asked for help.
As a team, Enzo and Wei now share the work fairly.

Ask your teammates for help when you need it.

Listen to others

Chip Cheetah's yoga instructor team is unhappy. Milly Monkey decides to complain.

I haven't had a break today. I'm very tired.

But Chip isn't listening.

When Omar Owl and Kit Kangaroo complain, too, Chip finally listens.

New team rule! Everyone takes a break between classes.

Chip learned a lesson. Now he knows that listening shows he cares about what his team has to say.

Listening is an important teamwork skill.

Talk to each other

Oh no! The restaurant orders and takeaway orders at Peter Panda's Pizza are all muddled up.

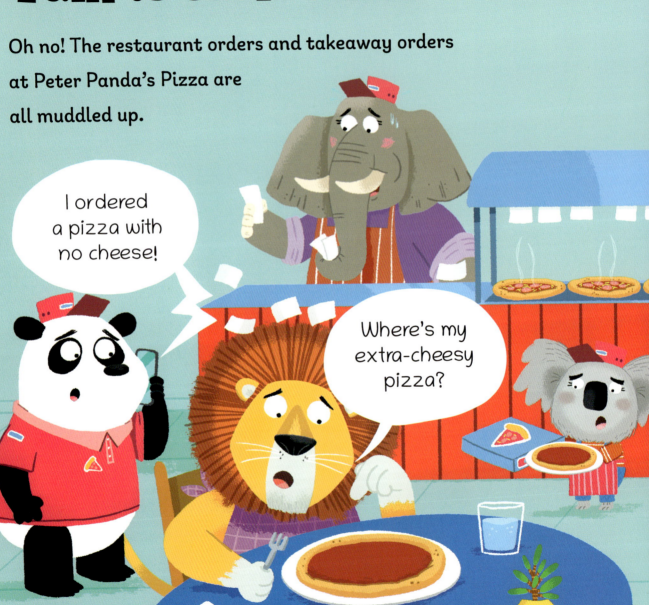

Peter Panda's team members talk to each other to work out a plan. Together, they decide to put the takeaway orders and the restaurant orders on separate piles.

I'll tell you when orders are ready, too!

Great idea, Enzo!

Talking helps a team to be organised.

Share your ideas

Tilly Tiger's trainer design team is very creative. But Tilly thinks that sharing their ideas could be great for her business.

Milly Monkey's trainer design is cool. Chip Cheetah's trainers are red. And Pip Penguin's trainers have flashing lights!

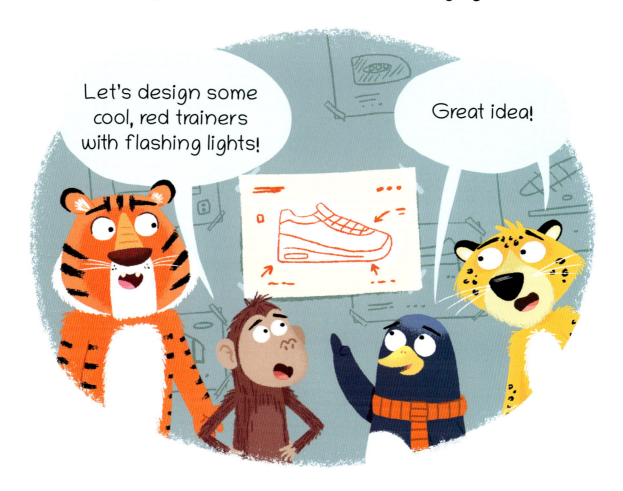

Tilly Tiger's team members inspired each other. Sharing ideas is fun!

When you share ideas, the whole team benefits.

Trust your team

Wei Wolf is annoying his Top Hats team.

He keeps checking up on them.

Then, Wei Wolf
realises something ...

My team never let me
down. I should trust
them to do their jobs.

He stops annoying them
and they finish all
the hats an
hour early!

Trust helps a team to work well together.

Know what to do

Pip Penguin and Kiki Koala are confused. They both think it's their job to serve the drinks in Kit Kangaroo's café.

We don't need more drinks, we need food!

Kit Kangaroo's team needs to know which job each animal does, so that they don't get muddled up.

Kiki, you serve drinks. And Pip, you serve food.

With Pip Penguin and Kiki Koala working well together, the café is running perfectly!

Knowing what you need to do is great for the whole team.

Welcome new people

Omar Owl decides to hire Leon Lion to help him run his kite-making business.

Leon is an expert kite-maker in his home country of Kenya.

Omar Owl's team is impressed. They haven't seen a kite like this before. Leon Lion's kite inspires them to try new designs of their own.

New ideas help my team to be more creative!

Welcoming new people to your team helps everyone to try new ideas.

Team up

A very important customer has ordered a snow statue. It will be the biggest statue Peggy Polar Bear's team has ever built!

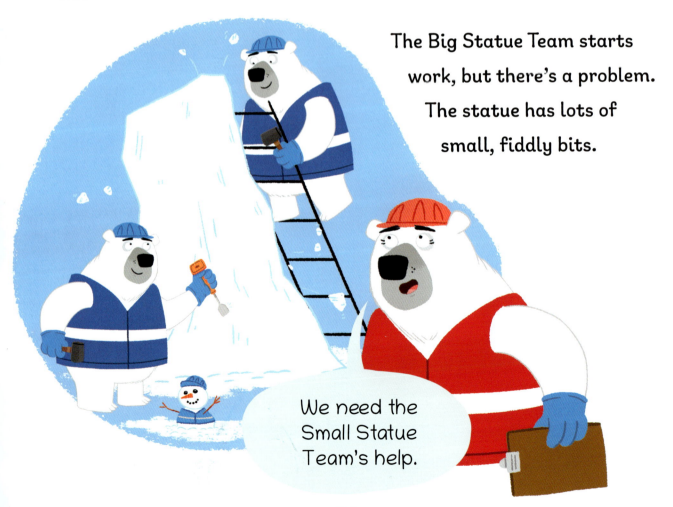

The Big Statue Team starts work, but there's a problem. The statue has lots of small, fiddly bits.

We need the Small Statue Team's help.

The two teams work together – and build
an amazing statue!

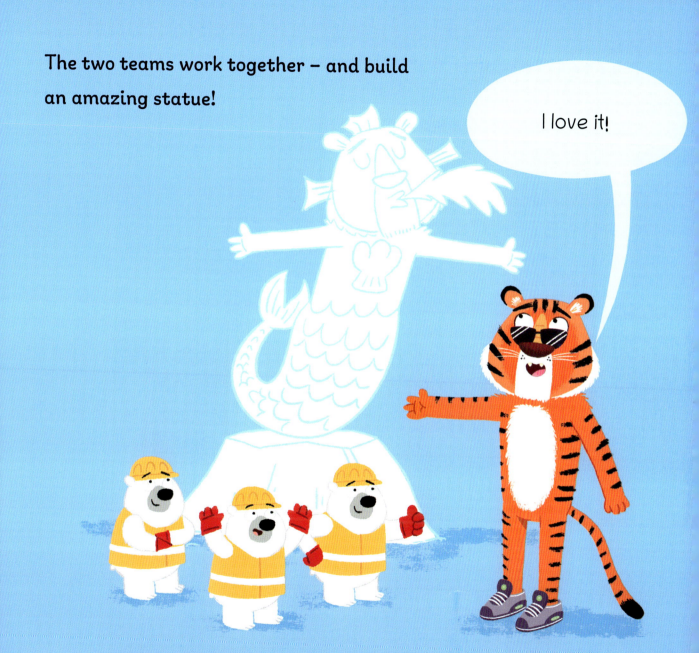

When you team up, you can solve problems together.

Succeed together

Kiki Koala's tree farm business is expensive to run.

One day, Kiki sees bees buzzing around the trees.

This gives her an idea.

Enzo pays Kiki rent money to put his beehives on her farm and open a honey shop.

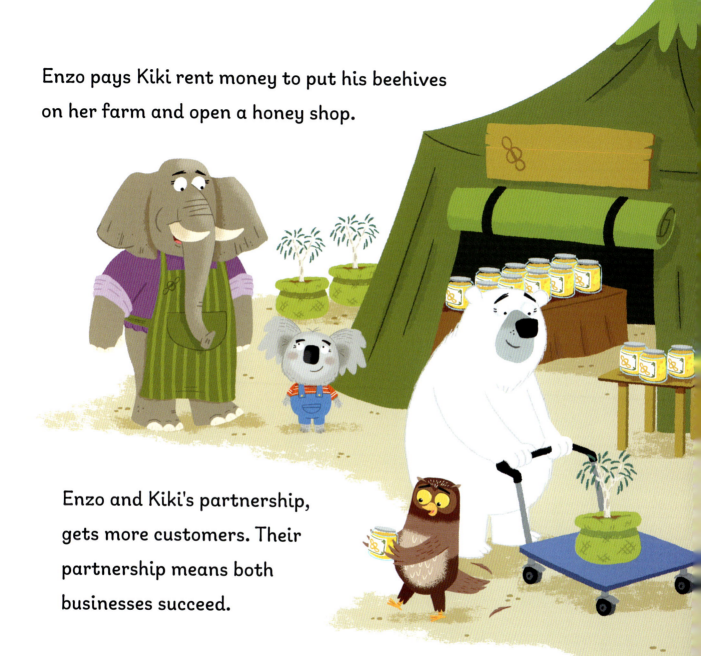

Enzo and Kiki's partnership, gets more customers. Their partnership means both businesses succeed.

A partnership is a way for two teams to succeed.

Reward success

Leon Lion's Roarsome Cars sold lots of cars this year. Leon gave himself a sports car to celebrate his success.

Leon thinks his team members must be very pleased about his success. But they are not!

Oops! Leon Lion forgot that success is down to the whole team. He gives them a sports car, too.

It feels good to celebrate success with your whole team!

Teamwork and you

Our animal friends have learned a lot about teamwork in business. What they have learned can help you, too!

Chip Cheetah listened. Listening shows that you care about others. Listening can help to solve problems, too!

Tilly Tiger's team shared their ideas. Sharing ideas is fun and inspiring.

Omar Owl welcomed someone new. Being new to a team can feel scary. If a new person joins your team or class, always try to make them feel welcome.

Notes for sharing this book

This book introduces business ideas around the topic of teamwork, which link to core personal and social teamwork skills, such as listening, trust and collaborating.

Talk to the child or class about what business is and why we need good businesses. You can use each scenario to discuss teamwork themes. For example, talk about how the child feels when taking part in group activities.

Teamwork succeeds when we are open to new ideas and experiences. Teamwork also relies on trusting others and speaking up. Talk about a time when the child worked on a class or group project. Did they enjoy being part of a team, or learn any new skills, such as being a team leader?

Glossary

benefit an advantage or an improvement in something

business a company that buys, makes or sells goods or services to make money

choir a group of people who sing together

customer someone who buys things from a business

expert someone who is very skilled at something; someone who knows a lot about a topic

fiddly something that has a lot of detail; something that is hard to do

hire to take on someone to work for you

inspired to feel like you want to do something

motivated to feel enthusiastic about doing something

partnership when two or more businesses work together to help both succeed

rent a payment made so that you can use something that belongs to someone else – such as a house or land

responsibility the things you have to do as part of your job

succeed to reach a goal